THE LORD OF EVERYWHERE

The Lord of
EVERYWHERE

poems · JOHN HODGEN

LynxHousePress
Spokane, Washington

Acknowledgments

Some of these poems originally appeared in the following publications:

AGNI: "Measure for Measure"

Alaska Quarterly Review: "Shark Week," "Ismael"

The Antioch Review: "Prime Movers," "Hamlet Texts Guildenstern About Playing Upon the Pipe"

Crazyhorse: "The Busy Griefs," "For My Father, Constant Soldier in That Vast Army of Men Who Have Claimed and Avowed With Absolute Authority That They Have Never Won a Goddamned Thing in Their Whole Goddamned Lives"

Green Mountains Review: "Accelerant"

The Nice Cage: "Accelerant," "Shark Week"

The North American Review: "Time Was"

Ploughshares: "Upon Reading That Among the Twenty-Five Thousand Pages of Love Letters That Passed Between Alfred Steiglitz and Georgia O'Keeffe Over a Period of Thirty Years, He Had Once Confessed to Her That He Had Wanted to Photograph Her Throat," "Watertown Man Charged With Manslaughter in the Drowning Death of His Best Friend"

Poetry: "Forget-Me-Not"

The Sun: "My Father's Hammer"

Willow Springs: "Jesus Tree," "Twenty-two"

Additionally, "Hamlet Texts Guildenstern About Playing Upon the Pipe" has been chosen for inclusion in Scribner's *Best American Poetry 2017,* and "Time Was" was a finalist for *The North American Review* 2017 James Hearst Poetry Prize.

FIRST EDITION

Front Cover Photograph by Noah Berger (Associated Press), "Delta Fire in Northern California"
Back Cover Photograph by Gordon Ripley, "Fall Sunrise on Mount Monadnock"
Author Photo: Robert Steele
Book & Cover Design: Christine Holbert

LYNX HOUSE PRESS books are distributed by the University of Washington Press, 4333 Brooklyn Avenue NE, Seattle, WA 98195-9570.

Library of Congress Cataloging-in-Publication Data is available from the Library of Congress.
ISBN 978-0-89924-16-5-4

*For Doreen, Janice, and Christie, for all those who have been kind to me,
and for everyone to whom I should have been kinder.*

Table of Contents

neither death, nor life . . .

nor angels . . .

nor principalities, nor powers . . .

nor things present, nor things to come . . .

nor height, nor depth, nor any other creature . . .

neither death, nor life,

Accelerant

I am cleaning out a woman's underwear drawer,
a woman who burned herself to death in the woods last week,
a woman I barely knew, whom I met maybe twice,
a woman my brother almost married twenty years ago,
but then said no to, slowly closing a door,
saying that in his honest heart, in that place he built
for himself like Lincoln's lonely log cabin,
that he loved her, but was not *in love* with her,
my brother for whom I would do anything,
who has told her broken family he would clean out her place
because they could not,
my brother who has been here for two days now,
whom I have imagined rummaging through her disembodied belongings,
going back and forth to the dumpster each day like Silas Marner,
my brother who has told me what to do to get started this morning,
this particular bureau, these drawers, how it all needs to be thrown out,
my brother who is in the shower now, who will come out in a while,
red-faced, quiet, who will see the rubbish bags,
the bureau, the empty drawers stacked up like little cribs,
and who, without a word, will gently lift up his side,
tilt it toward me as I carry my end down the stairs,
lug it out the door, into the morning light.

Enough

Enough to find them in the place they had crawled.

Enough to lift them into the transport vehicle,
take them to the lab, unzip the body bag,
slide them onto a slab.

Enough to poke and prod,
list cause of death (exposure, mostly, over and over),
this arm partially chewed, the bloated tattoo on the shoulder,
the masked faces of Comedy and Tragedy, the inscription
!Sonrie Agora, Llosa Despues!, dental records, DNA,
personal effects, rosary beads, communion cards
(*Benedicion, San Judas Tadeo*, The Prayer to Find Work),
the nub of a pencil, and, sewn in the shirt, the 100 peso bill
with the picture of Nezahualcoyotl, Hungry Coyote, poet and warrior,
who encountered the Unknown and Unknowable Lord of Everywhere,
and built a temple that remained empty for a hundred years.

Then to Missing Persons, then sit and wait, make every effort to identify,
repatriate, to Guatemala, Panama, Our Lady of Guadalupe,
then back in the bag, in a drawer with the others in a refrigerated room.

Enough for a day, shut the light, lock the door, and finally go,
toe tag, toe tag, John Doe, John Doe.

But at night they keep crawling toward the corners of our eyes,
their small fingers leaping like gifs, like vines around the irises,
saying one more mile, just over that rise.

And tonight in Manchester, New Hampshire, a woman, 60, laid off,
legally blind, has taken her life, has set herself on fire in a forest,
her condo foreclosed, a space now, empty, as if for a hundred years.

Enough, perhaps, if you only kept crawling, another seven hundred miles,
past Pima County to Old San Antone, then up through St. Louis,
past the crushed armadillos on Route 66, then right
at what's left of Detroit, past the packs of wild dogs,
up to Erie, Lackawanna, then all the way here.

There would be a space tonight, a quiet room, a temple of sorts,
enough, perhaps, with all the other missing, with all that is left
of the Known and Unknowable, the Lord of Everywhere.

Watertown Man Charged With Manslaughter
in the Drowning Death of His Best Friend

Fooling around, witnesses said, the man pushing his friend off the dock

with his foot when he couldn't wake him up. Svedka bottle back and forth

all afternoon, the one passed out, the other working him, cajoling, needling

wheedling, that if he didn't wake up, *wake up right now*, he was going

to push him in, thinking in his own wending, veering way, *promise cramm'd*,

as Hamlet said, as Svengali lived, and in the way bad vodka, bad movies,

and the intractable night make us think, that the water would jolt him,

revive him, that his friend would rise, surprised, from the river, like Venus's half

shelled drunken brother, shaking his hair, righteously pissed, calling him

bastard, son of a bitch, then suddenly laughing, finding a tiny golden fish

in his pocket, and thinking life was indeed that magical, comical, terrible,

horrible, like some forgotten Biblical parable, like cartoons, Stooges

or Pokemon Go, that we're all fidget spinners, all made of rubber, pixels, risible light,

capable of bouncing back, Gumby-like, to this world again, upright and forever,

like weebles, wobbly, inflatable punching bag clowns, wily coyotes, Truman Capotes,

like Jesus freshly baptized, 5-hour-Energized, coming out of the tomb, but with lawyers

this time, actually knowing Jack Shit, starting each day all over again,

re-inventing the world, no fooling around.

While the other, wet Lazarus, his bud, his boy, his restless other heart,

his little canoe, was drifting, slipping under the inexhaustible waves,

merely that, like a dreaming boy kept after school in seventh grade,

the teacher going on and on, the boy not asking for much, really, saying *Jesus, Jesus*,

under his breath, his plaint, his prayer, the gift that he longed for even more than the air, knowing for certain only what was real, what was there, that no one was coming

in his place, in his stead, that each given day was another kick in the head,

just wanting a little more sleep, just wanting to be left alone,

just wanting to wake up dead.

Jesus Tree

He's at it again, Jesus, his face showing up lately like manna on sandwiches,
potato chips, on bagels and cinnamon buns, in the steam on the windows at Subway's,
and this week in Flint, Michigan, in the crook of a tree outside the soon-to-be foreclosed
home of Ron and Marilyn Bielak, who need $84,000 to keep their house, who can't afford
 a lawyer, who come out slowly, guardedly, leaning against each other, like the true halt
and the lame, the cursed, the blessed, the trespassed against, to talk about their Jesus tree.

You can tell they believe. You can see it in their rivered eyes even before the reporters arrive,
that they've seen Jesus gone wild in the walled streets of Jerusalem, driving out the laymen,
money lenders, knocking over tables, even the squabby benches of the men selling doves.
They've seen him curse out a fig tree, watch it wither and die, then turn to his paparazzi,
tweeters, and snappers, to say that that was nothing, that if they wanted to they could tell
a mountain to throw its perfect self into its lonely brother, the sea, and if they had faith,
the faith of a mustard seed, for the love of God, it would damned well come to be.

Ron and Marilyn are saying *things will work out*, that we all will see,
that doves will come, *believe it*, to rest like moonleaves in their Jesus tree,
that mountains, many mountains, are moving to the sea.

Soliloquy

Nature finds its way, of course, inevitably, almost imperceptibly,
like a cosmic namesake more substantial, richer than we'll ever know.
This burnt sienna moss, for example, growing as it's always known how to grow
on the bifurcated measured blocks along the stonewall separating the property
of the residents of Main South in Worcester, Massachusetts, from the newly
constructed Dunkin' Donuts below. Here the Friday afternoon drunks show
up to brace themselves for the night ahead that will always come and surely go.
That and the cracks that already grow in the wall, that *no, no, no,* the way they know
how to pull stones apart, like separating children. But the afternoon light, *there,* just so
on the moss, translucent for a moment, ultrabright, the light the drunks hold tenderly,
like the last coin left before the cold, the oncoming night, Nature's legal tender currency,
its coin of the realm, its eye of Horus, *annuit coeptis,* its red tribe, blue tribe democracy,
its declaration, its signature, its shining city, when we can look at each other, fearlessly,
at our pupils, our irises, the haloed light inside our eyes that everyone can see.

The Harrows

On the commuter flight lifting up over Keokuk in March the visiting professor flying home
from the linguistics conference could see that the farmers had begun with their harrows.
And he thought, former clodhopper that he was, childishly, flippantly, what a harrowing
experience. And he thought how few people, except those in the checkered flat squares
of the flyover states, knew anymore what a harrow even was. Maybe the farmer's son,
 which he had been, and was, though probably he would not have known it then, only having
time perhaps at the end of the day to guess that it had something to do with harvests or rows.
And he'd have been right to a degree, though no teacher was ever going to ask him that,
the boy wanting only to get out of being the farmer's son, to be excused somehow, pardoned,
wanting it so badly that he schemed about it at night, feeling the dirt still stuck like stones,
like sticks under his fingernails before he fell off to sleep, grinding his teeth, wanting
with all he had, only that, another life, not knowing yet that that's what life was,
being cut open and lined into rows. The way we all feel now. Harrowed.

For most of us, if asked about harrows, on Jeopardy or Price is Right or Family Feud,
flummoxed for a moment, embarrassed, clickers in our hands, we might think we misheard
Alex, thinking arrows, perhaps, or Harrod's in London, Harrah's in Vegas, or Franco Harris,
or someone we knew once named Harold, Harold and Maude, or the old joke about God,
that His name might be Harold, Harold be thy Name, or Hark, the Harold Angels Sing.

Or this, if we live long enough, how it all starts to glow, how the earth and the words we were
made from, the black clumps of loam, were rich with the rain, the wind, the scattered seed,
the light, the shoots, what dies, what grows, how some of us made it and some of us didn't,
all of us harrowed into ribbons and rows, the bleached and narrow scarecrow leaning
at the edge of the field all alone with the harrier hawks and the harridan crows.

Upon Reading That Among the Twenty-five Thousand Pages of Love Letters That Passed Between Alfred Steiglitz and Georgia O'Keeffe Over a Period of Thirty Years, He Had Once Confessed to Her How Much He Had Wanted to Photograph Her Throat

He meant the neck, of course, that little chapel between what we feel and what we say,
that nave, that sacristy, where we are most vulnerable, always sticking our necks out,
like deer at the edge of a clearing, like a fawn reaching up to nuzzle the mother world.
For who but doctors or poets, William Carlos Williams, perhaps, could picture the throat itself,
that hollowed tree, that open boat, that red wheelbarrow left in the barnyard of the body?
Who can see into that darkened well, where on the surface float, like fallen leaves,
the words the heart has made? There as well the words we've never said, the ones
held close, gone dead, the breath taken in that dies its little death before we gasp or pant,
that rises up again, extant, to drift among the particles and motes, its groatsworth,
its little note, its Dickinson bird of hope within the open throat of the world.

Perhaps when our hearts are full, our hands held softly to our throats, like lilies in May,
we can see each other that way, like Steiglitzes of love, the loved one fully observed.
Look. There you are, at Thanksgiving or graduation or another wedding,
standing, a little tipsy, between your sisters for a photograph. And you are leaning
toward one of them, to nuzzle or kiss her, your neck arched, extended, exposed,
in pure, full-throated joy. And the words in your throat, if we could only hear them,

take their picture, would be what deer would say, the words we wait our lives to hear,
that now, right now, it is almost too much to bear,
that now, at this very moment, you have never been more beautiful.

On Wishing St. Augustine and Jimi Hendrix Were Here

Tonight I'd bring them both back if I could,
to watch this video, "Another Night in the Hood,"
in which a fight breaks out in a gas station in Chicago, South Side,
in which a righteous woman is rendered nude, is shamed and possibly glorified,
and in which one may also see the death of poetry, country, and all that once was good.

I'd ask them to sit on a funeral couch with me, one on either side,
as if watching *Antigone* or *The Simpsons* after all these years, to simply abide,
hands on their knees, to be comfortable, even manspread if they so decide,
as Augustine did as a young man in the baths of Tagaste, arousing his father's undue pride
at seeing his son's involuntary erection, his *inquieta adulescentia*, insisting, like a rising tide,
like Jimi's Fender Stratocaster, Augustine's father thinking grandchildren, smiling wide.

We would watch as if watching *Our Town,* the gas station as proscenium perfectly framed and lit.
We would look as if at Edward Hopper's gas station painting, or the one in which his wife
would sit
nude as the world on a bed, her body filling up with the light coming in through
some immaculate
window, some realm beyond our reach, shining like God's gas station, its bright red pumps at
the twilit end of a highway at the ocean's edge, which is, in truth, the beginnings of the infinite.

Truth in the video as well, truth as violence, as pornography, a woman, strong, heavy-set,
arguing at a gas station at the end of the world, with two young men, boys really, still wet
behind the ears, someone's grandchildren, lost, falling down drunk, like the night,
    not knowing yet
how to be men, suddenly swinging at her, trying to kick her. And she erupts, knows how to get
busy right away, knocks them both to hell and back, humiliates them, a night
    they will never forget,

but in so doing loses her *kitenge*, her dress falling apart. She is naked underneath, like a marmoset, like Hopper's wife, infused with her rightness, her dignity. She vanquishes them utterly, no regret, picks up her dress, walks back to her car, head high, fierce as Clytemnestra, proud as free Tibet.

And so, unstable heart, sinner and saint, what say you, Manichaean Christian, man possessed, blessed with heaven's joys, to which all things rise, with all that you have not, and all you have confessed? And you, Jimi, magician, who chopped down mountains with the edge of your hand, even Everest, and who once placed your mojo member in a plaster cast because groupies asked you to, obsessed with the unholy notion of a museum of rock legends and their physical attributes as a palimpsest of diversity, saying you would be the Penis de Milo, that they would attest that you were the best, after Gatsby's New World trees were all cut down at the edge of the shore, that *fresh green breast*.

Who can see it, daresay it, that the death of one's country can be swift,
the death of the mother, the death of one's child, like Adeodatus, God's gift.
Praise Venus at the Half Shell Station. Hail her triumph, her greatness, her girth.
Wrap her in raiment, lift her, woman never to be named, electric lady of the fallen earth.
Come back to us now, Voodoo Child, Lord of Grace. Find us in this broken place.
Build us again. Play for us. Pray for us. Show us our future, our fate.
Or meet us on the next world. *And don't be late.*

American Airlines

The gate announcement in Terminal A comes on repeatedly, mechanically, institutionally,
a woman's voice, weary, muddled, each word a morphine drip hanging over a cliff above
the sea. No one's listening, her voice looping like a snake, like gauze wrapping slowly
around our heads. She's saying that American Airlines has opened a new lounge for people
in uniform, that service members can go to the end of the terminal to a room across from
Lost and Found. Lost and Found, she says, again, and in that moment she is Dylan's Isis,
the Oracle at Delphi, the Mother of Imminent Doom. And soldiers are crawling, serpentine,
escaping, evading to a service members lounge. Other soldiers report directly to Lost and Found,
where they stand like the terracotta warriors in the mausoleum of the first Qin Emperor,
like an army of the afterlife, like the ghosts of the stones they have become. But here,
suddenly, a small boy runs halfway around our seating area and comes to a stop.
He shimmers, shudders in absolute delight. He looks as if he is about to explode.
He is so filled, so utterly round with happiness it is as if his joy will spill out of him
if he leans either way. He is like a clay rainwater vessel outside a temple in Bagram
when the earth begins to tremble. His eyes lock on his mother behind me. He is playing
hide and seek. He leans left. He leans right. He is lost. He is found.

Bereavement Rate

I ask the airline representative what I need to do to fly bereavement rate.
She looks up, says she's sorry for my loss, shows a delicate
combination of poise and reserve that might, at the very least, indicate
that she's gone through this before, which I tell her I appreciate.
She says it's a simple process, a form to fill out so they can authenticate
the name of the deceased, essentially the time, the place, the date.
I want immediately to ingratiate myself, but tell her I have to complicate
this a bit, that I truly hate what I'm about to say, that I want to compensate
her somehow for what she is doing, give her a discount commensurate
with what she has to go through each and every day, to endlessly state
the policies, the corporate protocol for what's ostensibly the going rate
for living and dying. She looks away. I realize that I'm starting to perseverate.
I hesitate, then out myself, say what I need is a permanent bereavement rate,
that I'm carrying too many deaths with me lately, like Atlas cursed, the weight
on my back like a dead man's carry, that I am Death's corpsman, medic, bosun's mate,
that I am not here to berate, to cheat, nor to vitiate,
that each day I am consigned to lift the bodies of those who've been killed,
Death's contraband, its heavy freight,
that I feel as if I'm trying to free them from this place, the newly dead,
the aggrieved, the aggregate,
but I can't carry them all anymore, that they're all outside right now, that they
all need the bereavement rate,
that I've been trying to teach them to levitate, transubstantiate, congregate
in some cumulus cloud, some school in the sky where they can integrate,
graduate, the kids killed in class, the deaths by cop, the victims of state
sponsored terror, the drive bys, suicides, asylum seekers made to wait,
the dead refugee boy washed up on the beach, like a baptized initiate
who has learned that to be drowned is his religion, his fate, to elucidate,
prevaricate, to become deadweight, his body like a tiny shipping crate,
as if a coffin had fallen off death's transport ship from Kuwait,

his face on the sand, how with each wave his flesh will tear, abrade, ablate,

and though he is filled with the weeping of the Mediterranean, I can lift his awful weight,

but the children here now forced to separate,

not dead yet, but dead inside, in the waiting room of the vacant heart, inviolate,

each like an ancient mariner, the body of the other hanging from their necks

like an albatross, a counterweight,

each breath like a rhyme, riven, like an unlatched, rusted prison gate

swinging forever between the bereaved, the bereaved, and the hate, the hate.

Pale Beauty

Today at the window, that Hellespont, open chapel for every poet,
a white moth flies by, *campaeea perlata,* pale beauty, hinky, herky-jerk,
as if a flower learning to fly, broken free of phylum, floss, skittery, jittery,
all stops, starts, stick-shifting, like the third Wright brother, wrong right,
half-right, left behind, having somehow found his way to the midst of the air,
now fraught, crying *mayday,* having no idea how to land. Or those Vaught Corsair
fighter planes my father made in the Second World War, but could not fly himself,
his back polioed, humped, like a flower pot handle, the planes with the folding wings,
crammed onto carriers, like makeshift origami, knick-knacks, doo-dads, whim-whams
on a shelf, like *kitsch.* Or like Juliet's palmer's hands held out to Romeo, her *holy kiss,*
the planes that would roar and lift off the decks, all prayers to God and Pratt & Whitney,
drop completely out of sight for a moment, then rise, impossibly, *holy shit,* into blessed air,
the flight crews fully woke, joking, hoowahing, waving their arms, the planes making
their way to heaven or hell, as am I, painstaker, heartbreaker, on my way to meeting
my maker, rainmaker, haymaker, widowmaker. I can hear my gravemaker, singing.

Wisdom

No one ever goes out walking looking for wisdom in Watertown, New York,
at least not on a weekend pass from Fort Drum, and most definitely not if you have to stand in line,
but tonight a woman tells me that she once lost a nightgown in the city of Pisa, and we both lean
to the left and laugh, knowing that her story needs both a beginning and an end, and knowing
that's the way of it with wisdom, that it asks of us, that there is always some loss, some nakedness
required before wisdom can come, like *the wrath of the lion,* Blake says. And tonight I am thinking
of a Saturday afternoon years ago in Watertown, New York, one p.m., and already a line forming
outside the Watertown Hotel. A prostitute, someone said, her man going up and down the line
making change, saying it won't be long now, and she'll do anything, each man in line knowing
both nothing and everything, each one a story needing a beginning and an end, getting on, getting
off, the woman, her body a poor vessel on a dark and ragged sea. And some of us, my friends
and I, walking away, too dumb, too poor, too scared to stand in line, more shepherds than soldiers,
sore afraid, maybe hating ourselves, wanting to destroy our own bodies, drink ourselves stupid,
not be soldiers for a while, some of us, not me, who later would walk into cities like Hue and Saigon,
our sons now walking into Kabul and Kandahar, looking, still looking for anything but wisdom.
And this woman, as I imagine her, as I am reminded of her tonight, her eyes two lost moons
over the country of her body, where young men go looking only to hammer and get hammered,
where young women's bodies are pounded like veal, and where one can walk into the ruined heart
of a city, even Watertown, New York, and find, broken and bloody, what we can never know
or even name, what Randall Jarrell said in the night can only be pain, and call it wisdom.

nor principalities, nor powers,

Love Me, Do

Lawns scruffy, gone almost to seed, this side of the street,
shrubs turned to moptops, like dead Beatles on the Sullivan show,
my neighbors and I scuffling now, re-learning fertilizer, compost, peat,
doing it ourselves again, since the Lawn Guy died three weeks ago.

Suicide, the neighbors said. (Was it yesterday, the night before?)
Up to his ears, buried in debt, done in by every little thing.
We knew he was a taxman, worked at The Money Store,
had split with his wife, landscaped after work, his old car pulling
up, trailer hitched behind, his daughter with him sometimes, smiling.
How he let her drive his car, working hard eight days a week.

Oh! Darling, I want to tell you there's a place you can seek,
that you'll get back to where you once belonged, it's true,
that it gets better, it won't be long, that it's just you, you'll do.
Do you want to know a secret? (None of that is true.)

How did he lose sight of you, you, his own seed, so
like a flower that forty years ago he would've worn you in his hair?
How did we look through him, back and forth, row on row,
not see him standing a moment longer here by the stone wall, or there,
like a fool on the hill, or everywhere, like Eleanor Rigby, patient as a nun,
having lifted an enormous fallen branch, and tossing it right there,
like the weight of the world, like a walrus, like a warm gun.

Upon Waking to Find That Birds Have Shit on My Car Once Again, and Deciding, For This Day at Least, That I No Longer Live in a Country of Beauty and Women and Men, and Upon Hearing That Lucy Has Died, My Grumpy Nun, Brave as Hell, Honest as the Day She Was Born

I live in a country commandeered by birds.
They fly commando, *de offendendo*,
like baldheaded *Apocalypse Now* Marlon Brando.
I am tired of their accuracy, their artillery, their turds.
There is no beauty in guano.
I want them all to go back to Capistrano.
Shit on them for a while.
That would make me smile.
That would rock my world.

All I know of my world today is that Lucy, 94 years old, has died at 4:30 this morning,
a woman who had cried out to her doctors for weeks that she hurt "down there."
"In my womb," she said, moaning even in her sleep, "Nurse, nurse,"
into the ambient hallway night, her cries so broken, so wounded, so deep,
that if the nurses hadn't come eventually, like somnambulist sisters from hell,
to give her more morphine, the walls themselves would have begun to weep,

her cries echoing, morphing, unimaginably, into *worse, worse*,
like some tormented wake of vulturous birds, then devolving, shuddering,
like the pictures of her grandchildren falling off the walls, into *curse, curse*,
the doctors like blind miners tunneling under the lost countries of the earth,
dead canaries all around, strewn about underfoot, until they discovered her vein, her brain,
her kidneys shut down, her death yellow skin, the vaginal tumor the size of a bird's nest.

This morning I am sitting for a moment longer in the parking lot of a CVS.
I'm a red dot on a map. I don't know who I am. I don't know why I'm here.
I only know I'm done for a while, that this moment is mine. I am holding it
like Lucy's rosary, like the little bell she would use to call for help,
forgotten now, left by the bureau when they cleaned out her room,
the bell silent yet ringing just the same, for some church,
some country that did not know her name.

I'm staring at the two-storied CVS fortress wall, bellwethered, Jericho-strong,
the red metallic *C* and *V* and *S* drilled into the side,
and next to them, incongruously, the word *BEAUTY*, also metal and red,
also drilled into the wall, and there, within the curved and open bottom
of the letter *B*, just as incongruously, incredulously, a bird's nest.

I watch the birds flutter in, all ailerons, wind shear, reverse thrust,
and joy, to the place where they know they'll be safe for a while,
safe as immigrant Jesus, taken as a child into Egypt for asylum,
safe as Lucy, as I imagine her, at the airy boundary of heaven,
every bell ringing, Lucy stepping painlessly into some other world
for which on this earth, at this moment, there is no word.

Shark Week

She says she likes Shark Week, adjusts her schedule each time it comes around,
says it terrifies her in the most satisfying way, the room preternaturally dark,
the TV light coming at her as if from the shark itself, from its God eye, as if she's living
underwater, life circling constantly, then coming in, trying to kill her, honest, relentless as hell.
Just like God, she says, His steady dorsal fin. It is what it is, she says. It is the wages of sin.

She remembers in eighth grade swimming across Hawk's Pond with the others, panicking,
struggling mightily to quiet her breathing, each of them thinking they never would make it,
yet arriving somehow, trembling survivors, to drink what the boys had brought, shot after shot,
the whiskey wriggling inside her, constricting, like a fish that she swallowed, that snakes in her,
breaks in her still, the thing that she wakes to, clings to each morning as it slithers away.

Sometimes she remembers back farther than that, an old postcard her grandfather sent her
that she never threw away, an Indian in a canoe on a lake. Hiawatha, she thinks, staring
into the water, the water so still he could see his reflection, and then, even deeper, below,
a great fish underneath, the arc of its body exactly the same as the curved bow of the canoe.
Which is it, her grandfather asked her. Does the fish down below want to be us in the boat?
Or are we the ones swimming, catching our breath, always trying to be like the fish?

The Busy Griefs

for Sam Hamill

In 1694 Basho wrote of his regret for not allowing two prostitutes
who had mistaken him for a priest to accompany him
when he set out in the morning on the narrow road to the interior.
He told them that their faith would be enough to guide them.
Two frightened young girls left alone on the highway,
the man who had left them promising to mail their letters
to their mothers. Basho having overheard the two of them
whispering to each other of their fear the night before
in the shelter where they slept like moonlight on clover.

The two girls so aware that we wander like children
moving by chance on the beach where white waves fall.
Each of them so anxious, each day the next man they will meet.
At every turn, the crooked, hand-painted signs stuck in the sand,
places called *Parents Desert Children*, *Children Desert Parents*,
and *Turn Back the Horse*. Basho all alone turning in his sleep
in the temple. The weeping of the prostitutes lifting up
to the moon like all the lost poems in the world, each one
trying to get as far away from this place as possible.

Poem With a Last Line From Browning's "Thirty-Third Sonnet from the Portuguese"

According to Fodor's the Portuguese say truth is the most horrible joke of them all,
though I do not know if the Portuguese really say that over and over to each other,
except in their *fado*, their songs of sorrow, their *saudade*, or if they ever say it at all.
And I wonder what it is that Fodor's says Americans always say, something like *Whatever*,
or *Really?* or *I'm just saying*. What qualifies as a truth or joke that people always say,
something said childishly over and over, something that waits and will never go away?
Tonight there is a dead child lost somewhere along the southern tip of Algarve, Portugal,
and the footage of her is shown over and over, the endless loop exactly like a cruel
joke, her turning, slowly, smiling at the camera, her mother and father, caught walking
guardedly, again and again out of the courthouse, now suspects, persons of interest, looking
down, then at each other, jittery, helplessly, then far off to something only they can see, seeing
a land only Jesus has to see, its longitude of truth, its horrible joke, parents, children, the killing
that goes on, calling to each other by pet names, calling *Papa, Baby Girl*, ever sweet, inchoate,
the names themselves designating their held belief that there is no joke like that, no crueler fate.
Yes, call me by that name,—and I, in truth, with the same heart, will answer and not wait.

Twenty-Two

At twenty-two the army was to be Einstein's purlieu

had it not been for his varicose veins, those blue

constellations, and his feet, flat as andirons, one in each shoe.

And at twenty-two Petrarch fell in love, Dylan did too,

brazen and biased in Harvard Square, the sunny pastures, the howdy-do.

At twenty-two Pocahontas died, Sinatra was arrested, Caresse Crosby, of the Mayflower blue

bloods, patented the world's first brassiere, that soft sweet nest built for two,

Boswell met Johnson, Darwin set sail, Heifetz bought his Guarneri, "ex David del Gesu,"

Cassius beat Liston, Salinger was drafted, Hemingway went to Paris, Byron turned blue

crossing the Hellespont. And you, and you, twenty-two, everyone asking, *What do you do?*,

each day getting longer, the tightened thumbscrew, the *koo koo kachoo*, this rue for you,

this solid flesh, this pistol shot, this too, too. Adieu, adieu, the ululu, the constant queue,

your hair askew, the world untrue, the lhude singing goddamn cuckoo,

all or nothing, heart in your hands, whatever, love, what will you do?

Red Hillside, Pitiless Wind

In Willa Cather's "Wagner Matinee" a Boston Conservatory music professor,
thirty years old, elopes with her lover, a younger man from Vermont, an inveterate idler
with no prospects at all. They purchase eighty acres, at one dollar per,
in Red Willow County in frontier Nebraska, which they have to measure, plot, stake out for
themselves, tying a red handkerchief around the spoke of a wagon wheel, counting the number
of revolutions, then turning ninety degrees, plotting their property line, counting, turning, over
and over, counting again, till they make their new love, their new life into a square, him, her.

How intense, new love, red with beginning, that counting and turning, starting again,
each turn a preview of a day yet to come, the rich black loam on the wheel coming
up, the red handkerchief on the spoke going down. Her handkerchief, Boston linen,
the bright silk of every promise they had whispered to each other, in time turned
to rag, bleached with alkali, stuffed in a hole in the window of their dugout, the hole in
the ground where they lay, the lace fading more quickly with each turn of each day,
like the silence at the end of a Wagner Matinee, into terrible, terrible, terrible gray.

Break

December twenty-sixth, and already the grounds crew is taking down the crèche.
They place the shepherds, the caliphs, like crash test dummies, into separate crates,
then lift Mary, Baby Jesus, more carefully it seems, then Joseph, last of all, so patient,
dumb, that look on his face, still wondering if anyone is ever going to tell him
what's happening, that look that I know at this moment is not unlike my own.
I am the fourth wise man, least-wise, arrived too late, no gifts in hand, sore afraid,
worn to death, as Keats once said, *like a frog in a frost*, my love crashed all around me.

Now the boxes being stacked like coffins in the back of the pick-up truck, the crèche
itself being carefully tipped into the front loader bucket bay to be balanced, lifted up,
taken away. What can I do but follow this cortège, the manger on high making its way,
tractor speed, across the lot to the maintenance shed, to be stored, manger within a manger,
for another year. When they finish, the grounds crew, wiser now, sits for a while, disciples,
apostles in un-Christmasing, they seem so proud, so satisfied, as if they have each just left
work to make love to the woman of their dreams. One takes out a pack of cigarettes,
Marlboros, I think, but I wish they were Camels, the finest Turkish tobacco, the ones I'd walk
a mile for. He taps the pack, hands them around, like gifts, like love. In the half shadow
darkness in the back of the shed, and before they step out into the light again, their cigarettes
flare, one by one, like Jesus, Mary, and Joseph, like Keats, each its own bright star.

Tip

Even the hotel maid her lover is pushing himself into will never
be the same as she was changing sheets just this morning. She'll be forever
exhausted by the end of her shift, like the toilet with the broken tank cover
in 327 that never stops flushing, the next bed unmade, the duvet and bedcovers
on the floor like hell to pay, like a Christo installation. As he sighs above her,
says her name over and over, she looks to her left, is streaming the two lovers
on *Desperate Housewives* doing the same thing they are doing, recalculating,
like giant parakeets, or sculpture intertwined, like the *Laocoön*, coupling.

Love's always walking on, being made and remade until it starts dying.
Love puts in its two cents and then it stops trying. Love leaves when it's time.
Beauty, not love, that draws our interest, beauty in the business of being sublime,
finding someone's wallet fat with fifties on the street, staking its claim,
beauty a reserve, a transaction, an exchange, beauty a monopoly, a game,
not hotels, only banks, saving, giving thanks, beauty, not love, that's to blame.

On Passing a Middle-Aged Couple in a Hallway at the Cliff House in Perkins Cove and Realizing at One A.M. This Morning That I Hadn't Clearly Looked at Their Faces, That They Might Have Been James and Annie Wright, the Famous Poet and His Wife Who Saved Him, the Couple I've Been Reading About in His Biography, **A Life in Poetry,** *by Jonathan Blunk*

To be blunt it was probably the ridiculous puffy and checkered complimentary hotel bathrobes they were wearing, something I am certain my wife and I would have had trouble doing, as they walked back from the heated pool. It was their *differentness.* It wasn't that they were simply unfazed in the way some couples embraced wearing *I'm With Stupid* t-shirts with the arrows pointing at each other back in the day. It was their awareness, their *duende,* the sense that even though I had not looked directly into their faces, that they were abundantly present unto themselves, and to others, that they fully inhabited the space they were in, even dripping wet, that they were profoundly happy, that they might have even been glowing, spending eternity as saints now, one dead, one still living, walking comfortably among us, making poems of each of us, that that was the way the universe had actually functioned all this time without my noticing, that if I only had looked in their faces they would have been smiling, true *doppelgängers* of poetry and heroic love, they who so loved to swim, who swam each day in the Grotto di Cattullo in Italy during the last few months before he died, when poems came easily in the cafes each morning, or when they had stood together transfixed in the chapel of Saint-Sulpice in Paris under the Delacroix's mural of *Jacob Wrestling With the Angel,* that they would have blessed us, equally, we who live for this time under the reign of a madman, puffy and unchecked, who neither knows nor cares about anything beyond himself, neither poetry nor painting nor love, who lords over us, like an empty hotel bathrobe, we who are consigned to live for a time like Adam and Eve, exiled, denied asylum, forced to leave the Garden, or like Dante's pilgrims walking past other couples every day in Purgatory, couples not looking at each other, couples wrestling with demons and dangers and disasters every minute of every day, couples not glowing like saints, but totally engulfed, consumed, then born again relentlessly, in wildfires, in Paradise, in California flames.

More Reasons to Disbelieve

There's this. How Keats's friend, Charles Armitage Brown,
who let him down, who failed his friend so infamously,
could bollix love, refuse to glean what Keats had found,
sweet Fanny Brawne, his own bright star, his teeming sea,
could see their love as annoyance only, as a tiny thing,
as tsetse fly, *atom's atom*, a single drop of blood. There's this.
How love can kill, his friendship lost, how love can sing
at the dirge of the other, its toxic urge its own tuberculosis,
so strong it gets inside, destroys the lungs, its strict prognosis
to reign in the heart, rule mercilessly, a faerie queen, deeming
him pale knight, king of nothing, decreeing even that no birds sing.
And this. Erstwhile Keats coughing in a coffin, Fanny mourning,
Brown ghosting, crossing moors all alone, less alive every day,
friendless, lifeless, loveless, with holy hell to pay.

nor things present, nor things to come,

For My Father, Constant Soldier in That Vast Army of Men Who Have Claimed and Avowed With Absolute Authority That They Have Never Won a Goddamned Thing in Their Whole Goddamned Lives

The people he would tell:

Anyone, everyone, people in line at the bank,
wedding guests, the mailman, for God's sake,
Bill the barber, who cut what was left of his hair
close to the wood every Saturday afternoon for most of his life,
my drunk Uncle Harry, poker player, shot in the eye with an arrow as a kid,
or Oley Olsen, who played the ponies, ran the weekly pool, worked the counter
at the Hubbardston Package Store, where my father would stop on his way
to borrow money from his brother in Belchertown, Ike, the state rep,
but not until he had had three nips before he got there, slinging each bottle
out the window as he drove, then downing sardines out of a can to cover the smell.

Dead a year later, heart attack, losing everything then, curled on a cement floor
like a shepherd's crook, a shepherd, you can bet, who lost all his sheep,
whose dog had run off with the Ringling Brothers, the wolf in sheep's clothing
leaning against the wolf tree blowing smoke rings with my father's Camels, unfiltered.

Today, this photo in the mail, a gift, all of us on a couch at my uncle's,
my father flummoxed, bamboozled, gone to wrack and ruin, fallen once again
for the old flimflam, staring straight through the camera, his soul being taken,
the price of admission, as if he had doubled down, lost it all, the blue chips of his life
being pulled away slowly across the felt table by the smiling croupier, my father dazed,
crazed, as if he had asked for no blindfold at his own execution, as if he were Dostoevsky
staring at the rifles of his kinsmen lined up against him, thinking only *blue sky, blue sky*,
my mother, smiling, longsuffering, slowly playing out the slim hand she was dealt,
and the four of us, my brothers and I, sitting in the middle, looney as hell, mopes, dopes,
three time losers already, bright-eyed, bushy-tailed, everything aces,
convinced beyond a shadow of a doubt that we would win the world.

Albino

Who knows why these things happen, why we hold them all our lives, my father
waking us one night, telling us to get dressed, to come outside, and be quick about it,
my brothers and I, fuzzy-headed, half-dreaming, as he led us down the stairs, and out
to the moonlit garden, the soft earth fallen asleep under our feet, and then beyond.
Be quiet, he said. *Don't even whisper*, him with a flashlight, each of us stepping dumbly
behind the other, some tiptoe caravan, little troopers of the night, until we stopped,
bumped, and gathered around him as he motioned us to look where he was shining
the light. *There, right there*, at the edge of the trees, a group of deer standing, looking
straight at us, not moving away, a family, the little fawns pure white in the brightness
wafting around them, and then, miraculously, growing whiter. *Albino*, my father said,
very rare, we not even knowing what albino meant, the whiteness something we had never
seen, whiter than Jesus in *King of Kings*, whiter than the wide-eyed, pre-Neil Armstrong
moon, the deer eyes looking at us the same way we were looking at them, caught for
a moment, learning each other, the brightness sinking in, becoming love, what else?
And then they were gone, just like that, quick about it, the father sensing us, yearning,
then herding his family quickly into the darkness, the little ones trusting, leaping
soundlessly away. What we would know only later when we fell in love, each in our time,
fuzzy-headed, half-dreaming, as if we were standing at the edge of a clearing, and it was *there*,
right there, the earth giving way under our feet, love coming, then turning, then gone, *very rare*.

On Finding Two Love Letters from My Father to My Mother in the Same Envelope, Dated May 24th and May 25th 1944

The envelope:

"Postage due, 3 cents" in pink, hand-stamped, returned to sender for additional postage by some clerk, some functionary in the dead letter office, the rain and the snow, the letter needing to get to my mother, to her mailbox, her little silver house of waiting and love, the red flag tilting up, she and the baby now back at her mother's, my father finding work in East Hartford, Pratt and Whitney, making planes for the war, then hopping the train Saturday night to Hubbardston, Massachusetts, to spend all day Sunday with her.

My father, (how he would have handled it):

The swearing, of course, then the silence, no stamps in the house, the day that was lost, the letter like a child wandered off, brought back by the mailman, the three cents (the ones made of lead that year, the copper conscripted for the war effort, for the soldiers, for the casings for bullets, Abe on the front, the same color as a mailbox), the trip to the post office, the pennies dropped one by one in the cash drawer, the coffers, the great engine of love letters slowly churning again, love overcoming my father's steel rage, his anger harder than mail.

The letters:

The first one, the return address "214 Lonely Street," in which he calls her "little one," "sweet," and (twice) "wonderful one," and in which he tells her of the new moon that night, "silvery, slivery," but just right for them to sit upon while Peter the baby tries to catch his own star. He says he's no good at writing letters, says he can't stand another minute without her, says he almost came to her mid-week, asks if she would have been surprised to see him step from the train, as he intended to do the day the letter arrived.

The second, in which he says, "I love you" three times, and that he wants to feel her hand in his, that he thinks that the baby can hold both their hearts in his tiny hands.
At the end he tells her they will love each other, truly, for two thousand years, though one year, sadly, has already gone.

Both of them gone now, the post office too, my parents delivered, returned to sender, this envelope their sepulchre, their paper tomb, postage due, the letters still alive in my hands.

The Calling of Saint Matthew

In Strozzi's painting Jesus is calling out Matthew from the hedge funders,
the tax collectors, to walk off the job, leave the money on the table, switch to his team.
And Jesus really nails him, arm fully extended, pointing right at the coins of his eyes.
But even Jesus seems surprised, Jesus the upstart partisan, citizen soldier, the Goth kid,
emaciated, pale-faced and loony, filled with a frenzy he can't keep inside, as if he glows
in the dark, as if he caught fire, swallowed a hive, the aura, the aura, as if it's eating him alive.
Matthew, he says, *you have to come with me.* I want you, he says, in his best Uncle Sam.
And Matthew rears back, hand to his chest, afraid all the way to his shoes.

It's the hand on his heart that calls up my father, that thing he would do, caught at the table,
cards all around, drinking again, as if he were thinking his heart had slipped out of his chest,
that he wore it now like a blue frog thumping, like Diogenes' lantern, like Flava Flav's clock.
And the woman who approaches me today as if she's been wandering for two thousand years
who sees my heart on the outside too, knows I'm in the sad army, like her, like a wedding guest,
that I can't help but listen, hand on my chest. She simply begins, opens herself, each word
a new pearl of her sorrow. She says she can't talk with her mother, hasn't spoken for years.
She says she almost left work today, drove to the ocean, to feel the waves
that would cradle her, carry her away. I stare at her. She is a million miles away.

Me? I say, shrinking, *not me that you mean. Too old, now, too busy,*
all loopholes and fees. You must be mistaken, not me that you need.
You, whispers Jesus, *you're the one that I'm after.*
Jesus, I answer, *sweet Jesus, not me.*

Prime Movers

Who'll throw out all my stuff when I die, my huff and puff
my gaud, my guff? Some biff, some bindlestiff?
Who'll come down on my hold like an Assyrian?
Abou Ben Adhem? Question Mark and the Mysterians?
Someone refined, white gloves, like George Solti?
Or someone who looks like the viral arrest photo of Nick Nolte?

Who you gonna call? Who'll finger my junk?
Who'll answer the bell, roll off their bunk,
like Ghostbusters, Prize Patrols, grief counselors, cats?
Who'll be there for me like old sports, like Jay Gatz,
saying *Jesus, what did he save this for?* or *Look, a Euro.*
Who'll go through my chiffonnier? Who investigates my bureau?

And what of my body, all popeyed, soused, and olive oiled?
Who springs my slinky mortal coil?
Who tenders my body after I have broken it for thee?
Who finally lets me be?
Who tosses my books, drinks my wine,
holds a glass up to the light, saying, *This is truly divine.*
Who casts John upon the waters, *ipso facto*, Mondo Trasho, Pink Flamingo?
Who gets my board game at the rest home, raises her trembling hand, says *Bingo.*

Twelve

Even Jesus knew twelve was a good round number when having your supper or buying a round.
Odds pretty good, actually, that out of any twelve people only one would betray you, refuse
even to repay you. A world you could live in, eventually, a testament of sorts, safe bet,
even among all your cohorts, your posses, your crews, that most of us could survive an
odd evening out without having the screws put to us, being poisoned or stabbed.
Even our butter knives are laid out before us each night with the business ends facing in.
Even you would take those odds, that margin of error, short it if you had to, trust it would all
even out in the end. You'd think you could figure it, at least narrow it down, calculate the
odd one, Judas, there in the corner, drinking like a bastard, Thomas, dubious, taking you aside,
even sticking his hand in your wound, Peter, all promises, doing the dozens, dabbing, denying.
Even Stephen, later on, odd duck, figured he'd passed eleven others before someone said, barely
audibly, *That's him*, before they surrounded him, goddamned him, stoned him even unto death.

Forget-Me-Not

My brother is dying and I am not.
I drag him behind me like a spiritless balloon, like the first robot,
like the last clown car clown, his ridiculous Fiat, his lot
to be crushed, left for dead, covered in snot,
his puffy hands, his outsized shoes, his flower pot,
like Virgil Earp, Clanton-ganged, at the Not
OK Corral, un-brothered, gutshot,
like the night without sleep in Turandot.

From the get-go I have always sought
to know (what, *what?*) if this is all I've got,
to show up in a vestibule, all bothered and hot,
like silver-fingered Iscariot,
like the smiling highwayman, *tlot-tlot, tlot-tlot,*
while all about me are consigned to slather and rot.
I drink to my faith, to what I am not,
to all who've come before me, every rutty Lancelot,
every Huguenot, every hotsy-totsy hot to trot, every Dylan, besot,
who doesn't have the strength to get up and take another shot.
I know my Morse, code blue, *dot-dot-dot, dit-dit-dit, dot-dot-dot.*
I know what God hath wrought.

Early Onset: For My Brother

We are driverless cars, idiot automobiles, groundless, shiftless, upset at every turn,
some perfectly fine, German engineered, genetically DNA'd, made in shade, all set,
others poorly programmed, wires crossed, reset, to only drive in rain or park in sun.

What we need are balance sheets, some moral chronometer to measure the setting,
plot the course between Onset Point and Narragansett, between simple pleasure
and simply pain. We need set menus, Quakers, Shakers, more meat, more pudding.

We get, instead, a table badly set, knives and forks all widdershins, a Raft of Medusa
for every Santa Maria, an unsettled score, a wronged brother for every Wright. We're beset,
housetops on fire, mousetraps on every side. But you, your letter settled in my hand today,

welcome, warm, each word, each letter hard-won, like the inset letters on graves, a kind
of quivering Thanksgiving, a tiny, breathing Rosetta Stone,—especially the "*w*'s"—when you
wish me well—wiggly, wobbly, like wreaths, rosettes, riding waves on a wayward, wavering sea.

My Father's Hammer

After he died, my mother gave me his toolbox,
saying he would have wanted me to have it,
the hammer kept inside as if in a little grave.
When I take it out, holding its nicked and sweat-stained handle,
I feel as if I am shaking his hand, from those times he would come
to fix something, pound something back, make rough-hewn sense of the day.
I can still hear the rhythm of his hammering, that *tack, tack, tack*, as he struck
and swore at the rank disruptions of the world.
I hold those moments when he would nail a joist, pin it into place,
affix it, Mr. Fix-it, now gone for so long, with all the lost fathers,
dead as doornails, their hands so far away.
What a fix we're in, all the lost sons, our days, our nights,
like hammers lifted and hurled, lifted and hurled,
hammering, clamoring, at this heavy, inviolate, unfixable world.

nor height, nor depth,

I Have Seen It Go

I know thy works, that thou hast a name that thou livest, and art dead.

Call me Shackleton amongst the living, the dead, last to leave,
hard to bereave, amongst the mucky-mucks, the flora, the fauna,
the dourahs, the Donners, (something to chew on, no?)
wandering off now, against the grain, *about, my brain,* ghosting,
cool bastard that I am, muckled, un-mucklucked, into swaths
of swirling snow.

I'm standing weightless in the waiting room, Amundsen without amends,
amens, not even a men's room where I can go, like Osa without her Martin,
bishop without her queen, heart absent, fonder, eyes dried, cleaned out, sand for eyes,
pressed, like a heated sandbag held two years against my mastoid-
fevered ear, to render me, surrender me, toe-tagged, dew-ragged
Jane Doe.

I am expeditious Brutus, brutal, bootless, blue suede shoes under seven seas.
I render unto seizures. I'm all shook up. I'm vertigo.
I've gone to hell, visceral, vichysoisse, vitiate. (The fish he ate.)
I'm up. I'm down. I thrice refuse the thorny crown.
One for the money. *Et tu* for the show. Baby, please don't go.
I'm Petit mal, Petit
Charbonneau.

I'm double-parked, Lewis and Clarked, lost my Sacajawea, my worth,
my love, my life, unchained. The lights turned off. I'm all dressed up,
Shoshone-style, one tightly wrapped Arapaho. I'm rife. I'm feather-
brained, surrounded, Custered, mean Mr. Mustard.
I have no place to go.

Man of letters, last rider for the Pony Express, gone postal, my body
slung over the saddle, head stuffed in a haversack, pin-cushioned,

sent back, forty arrows Fed-Exed, Amazoned in my back.
But I've got ups. I'm still alive, alive-o.
Like Ahab, waled, bewailed, rope-a-doped, I lift my arm,
just so.

I call to you through the holes in my harridan heart, my open-year-
round, many-arteried Musee des Beaux Arts. I crawl out
from under bodies at My Lai, at Babi Yar, from under body parts,
the ones piled up, Bowie-knived, Burning Manned, at Jericho.
I can't remember the Alamo.

I am drunken, harried Don Quixote, pants around my knees, sun-blind,
punch drunk, windmilled, another dull sinner brought low,
like Hamlet's trappings and his suits of woe, his *that within which passeth show*.
I am fusty Lear, Chaunticleer, my daughters all dead, *no, no, no, no, no, no,*
no.

Bees in my hair, ferns wilding in my shoes, I jump from a plane,
truth be known, screaming everyone else's name but my own,
just to tell you the truth. No chute. No shitting. No bull.
I am lonely, free-falling
Geronimo.

Hooray for Captain Spaulding, the African explorer.
Did someone call me schnorrer?
Hooray, hooray,
hooray!

I am no explorer. I can't afford explorers. Call me Shackleton the alien,
a lot to prove, a far remove, as if I were Centralian, another jailed Australian,

the lone Episcopalian in a Catholic sea of hosts. I speak in glossolalian,
and this is what I say:

I am no Discovery. I am in recovery in an undiscovered country.
I have no true north, no star anymore. I decline. I have no azimuth.
I have no mother, though as a mother died I held her hand.
I have sat with her, only that, when her last breath ran out.
I have *longéd long*, as Ophelia has. I have shivered.
I have seen the light turn to grey in her eyes, a little river redelivered,

diverted, dried up, its meaning lost,
the last drop, the last tear gone
below.

I have seen the light she carried like a chalice,
like a chapel's perfect window in the center of her eyes.
It is a small truth, I confess it, that everyone must surely know.
But how it burns to know it is no longer so.
It does not make it easier. It does not make me wise,

the way a beaten child grows wise, that I have seen the light,
that everybody dies, that our lives are spent pretending, like Jo-
casta, hanging in the hood, that we live our daily lies, the fish we've
caught, the sun each night it dies, that only if we're deserving, or lucky,
like Plato, Pericles, *ex silentio*, or the Seventh Son,
even so,

or feckless, reckless, anodyne necklaced, John and Annie Donne,
that we can know the day we are undone, see the world within a room,
the light that lives in anybody's eyes, that we know is always there.
We know,

but still we let it go, like every sad-eyed Tuckahoe from Kokomo,
(I love you so),
every Old Black Joe, every racing heart Crowhurst, Lonely Crow,

clinging to our chronometers, jumping off the bow, craving fast or slow,
or leaping, leavened, like Icarus, from the top of cumulo-nimbus thundersnow
into the Auden-evened Bruegheled sea, with absolutely
no
one noticing, wandering to and fro,
to even look up to see if it was
or was not so.

It was so.
The blink. The wink.
The okey doke. The old I told you so.
The light we believed that would always be so.

I have seen it
go.

nor any other creature . . .

At 30,000 Feet

From here, top lit, the separate clouds cast shadows on the ocean,
like doppelgänger countries, continents, Cloud Atlases and Gazetteers,
New Zealand there, Africa over here, the entire United Shadow Nations,
the sunlight freely inviting Security Councils, ambassadors,
attendees to believe that the clouds themselves are inhabitable,
that life there ceding clouds might be possible, sustainable,
that those among us, poets, Shelley's legislators, with softened hearts
might be able to emigrate, repatriate, settle in these parts,
if we watched our steps, planted stakes, showed pluck,
in Cirrus Syria or Cumulus Namibia. What providence, luck,
to walk like Wordsworth, lonely, along the lakes, the banks,
or cloudy Keats, on Sandburg's cats feet, to show courage, thanks,
in April with Chaucer's *shoures sweet*, *corages*, to go on pilgrimages,
to St. Moritz or St. Cloud, like *gentil parfit* knights to pay homages,
to be set free like Birdmen of Alcatraz or Prisoners of Zenda,
to walk like Petit amid airless air, towering clouds, like holy Wallenda.
And if one fell, tumbling like Icarus (Audenless) or Earhart, to know
there was a shadow country perfectly aligned to settle into below.

Hamlet Texts Guildenstern About Playing Upon The Pipe

True that. Rue that.
That whch wld cause us 2 mscnstrue
that whch we alwys hve knwn 2 be true,
that we r a part of an unholy crew
that drms we cn do whtvr we do.
2 be honest eschw that. Chw that
fr a while. Msticate. Xpctorate.
Engnder only that whch will elevate. Do that.
Elminate that whch invites u 2 spculate,
pooh pooh that. Untrue that. Undo that.
At least try. Set ur azmuth 2 aim at what-
evr sky will allow u 2 prsue that.
And avoid at all csts the truths ur uncouth at,
squndring ur youth at, growng long in the tooth at,
7 a.m. drinkng vermouth at, 9 a.m. flyng to Duluth at.
Fnd that hue in the sky. Thn cry. Boohoo that. Hew 2 that.
True blue that sky course, that heart settng. Few do that. Sail 2 that.
And 2 anythng that wld skew that, u knw what to say. Screw that.

Despite Pharrell and The Rolling Stones's Repeated Requests for Them Not to Do So, the Trump 2020 Election Committee Continues to Play "Happy" and "You Can't Always Get What You Want"

for David Thoreen

It isn't the blatant and unauthorized repetition, nor the brazen crime of it, exactly,
more the impact, the pounding, each blow landing like a bone saw every way except precisely,
on *The Washington Post* journalist Jamal Khashoggi's fingers, then the arms and legs as well,
as if the screams each action induces would intensify exponentially, or modulate, even swell
somehow, almost happily, before the ultimate beheading. It's the lie, the double consciousness,
the deep shed malevolence of it, the snake charmer's charm, the shining cobra's lilt, the excess,
the people cheering long after the rally is over, believing that they can indeed get what they want,
that they can be great again, when they know in their driven hearts on the way home they can't,
that tonight at 2 a.m. they will park their Ram Charger, Avenger, F-150 or Dodge Caravan
under the carport next to the campaign sign that has been knocked down again,
the unhappy face on the sign like the moon having fallen, beheaded, the moon
looking up now like a dead man for his head, searching for the other moon.

Keats's Twins

Had it happened, as Goldbarth imagined, twin nightingales, *pair o' Keats*,
after his death, that posthumous existence, that second sight, sweet, sweet
Fanny sitting up in bed one night, one hand above, one below her heart,
that definitive movement, that sudden start.
Had she known, even in widow's weeds that she would carry two,
bride of quietness, her Grecian urn body, both beautiful and true,
she would have turned, instantly, her eyes, her inner eyes, toward the ocean,
the way we turn toward love, *happy misery*, taken and mistaken,
the way Keats said Cortez looked out upon the Pacific, when it was actually Balboa,
the way, knowing someone Biblically, we say Moses when we mean to say Noah,
the way all our heroes slowly turn into one, all our dreams become the same,
that meme that someone will remember us, will pass along our name.

But twins, both negative and capable, sweet memory, *sweet moan*,
would she not have taken them, together and alone,
hand in hand in her delight, to the shore, to point with them toward Rome,
Keats still there, of course, eternally dying, the Spanish Steps his home,
his blood going in, going out, like the tide,
her letters still unopened, held so close to his heart that now they were inside.

Would she not have walked them down to the edge of the water,
Keat's bright son, Keats's bright daughter,
rhyme and reason, one and the same, until they pointed too, confident and brave,
to say they could see him, at least his name, written on the tip of every wave.

Measure for Measure

At the Shakespeare colloquium on love and religion,
where the tables were clothed and squared together
to resemble four academic Last Suppers,
where, more precisely, at the first use of the word *Panglossian*,
and just slightly before the rejoindered collegial word *Neoplatonic*,
each like a gargantuan salmon leaping upstream within the linguistical river
of all the other words doing the best that they possibly could,
words such as *thumos*, *eros*, and *caritas*, amid the disciples waving their degrees
like dinner rolls, like selfie sticks, I doubted like Thomas, teetered like Judas,
fumed like Iago, and veered from candid devotion to countervailing belief
that I needed this exactly in the way that I needed another hole in my head.

And when I headed outside like a traitor, a varlet, a pox-headed minx,
like one needing an immediate and involuntary heart, lung, eye, and ear transplant,
I heard and then saw an oversized pileated woodpecker, hammering like a hanging judge
at a bald-pated oak tree that looked for all the world like Dante Alighieri wandered off
into the woods where bears go to shit. This, hours before I returned home to find two cords
of firewood piled high like a sawmill cathedral of blocks and stones on my neighbor's front
lawn, the load cantilevered, delivered, dropped so close to my tiny birch tree that it appeared
its bottom bark strips had fallen out of shock like a valance, like a miniskirt around its knees.

And slightly before seeing two colleagues from the morning session outside as well,
sitting at a picnic table in the snow, still speaking, but more ardently now, like errant
friars, Pangloss and Neoplatonic, like two new citizens drawn closer to what they
already knew, and what they would give of themselves later in the afternoon session,
he, magnificently bearded, head shaven, like a true prince of Verona, saying he had
awakened his wife that morning, called her *fair maiden*, and knew, for a certainty, that
Shakespeare was good for wooing. And she, her eyes dark and distinct as the small mole
just above the top of her blouse, the mole being, most probably, a *melanocytic nevus*,
a beauty mark, what the Romans called "olives of the body," which, if located on

the neck foretold a possible future beheading, and which medievals believed meant
the devil had entered the body, she, saying she loved her husband so much she could
never foresee a time when she would stuff a five dollar bill down a male dancer's pants.

Then the world came together again, and Shakespeare laughed like a midsummer's dream,
all of us standing and smiling at the end, the woodpecker thrumming, *thumos* and *eros*,
at the black mole of the universe, each of us wordless, glowing, a Pangloss about us,
measure for measure, like Claudio and Juliet, the only true lovers at the end of the play,
their child held within them, Neoplatonic, shining for us all for free.

Ismael

Ismael calls me, late, after eleven, Saturday night,
my carpenter who falls asleep in my class,
to say he has been thinking about what I said,
not that he is one letter away from a famous character,
but that he never speaks in class,
that he is as silent as some nameless sea
on the other side of the world.
He says he simply doesn't know what to say,
but that he wants to in his secret heart, that place
where he can safely rest, where he can stow away.
He says that the three hours grind him after work,
wave after wave, weighing on him like the roiling ocean.
He says he feels like he's the last sailor left on the dock
when the ship sails away, that ideas don't rise to the surface
for him the way they do for everyone else, easy-like,
like an albatross, or Noah's dove, having found an invisible world,
then coming in for a landing on a coffin, bevelled and sealed,
or on a hump-backed whale after it breaches,
coming to sit on its back so naturally, effortlessly, silently,

settling in, as if it were his long lost home,
as if it were the New World, bright ships all around,
lookouts in crow's nests waving madly and smiling,

everyone, everyone calling his name.

We Can Say Christmas Again

the police are out looking for jesus again
the kid down the street, the one they can't find

his mother holds pictures up high for the cameras
for the star, for the globe, for the herald to sing

she has her own lawyer, has been down to the station
has reportedly flunked her third polygraph test

(his father alone as the moon in the window
says he doesn't believe that drugs were involved)

we follow the cops down a network of alley ways
live feeds and lead-ins and back-ups at roadblocks

they say have you seen him, they're dragging the river
digging in graveyards, great stones rolled away

but jesus is risen, he floats on the water
wound in his side, dead for three days

and mothers go by holding children like presents
and mary nods off on the street getting stoned

and children are out playing dead in the leaves
and neighbors are canvassing subways and bars

and shelters fill up like cathedrals for thieves
and wise men leave town sore afraid of the stars

Time Was

One could tell just by looking, before the light would change, which hobo, grifter,
or stumblebum standing at the regular Friday intersection of Park and Pleasant
or Franklin and Main with the folded sign saying *Anything Will Help,* or *Homeless Vet,*
was authentic enough, had enough honest dirt on his shoes, or ragged hole in her shirt,
that we could build a story around, or that vague *weltschmerz,* that generic world weariness
in sufficient amounts, to avoid the just-going-homers getting all judgy, their eyes turning gray,
rolling the window down, giving the finger, hollering *"Get a job"* or *"Fuck you,"*
before the light turned red again, before they pulled away.

But tonight, storm coming in, an astral heaviness you can actually feel, heat lightning
in the distance, that green and yellow window dressing at the bottom of the sky,
and it's all transformed somehow, a kind of homeless Homecoming Weekend,
and they're all deserving as hell, broken beyond even Thomas's doubt. All of them,
especially her, the missing teeth, the bruises on her face, the scarecrow flophouse hair,
the zombie walk, the piss-stained, sweat-stained, hoobastank stink of heroin and fentanyl
in the air, that has me turning around and driving back, twice already in what feels
as if it could become some endless loop, some grooved track, again and again,
some crumpled tithing of fives and tens. Until she speaks, in a voice I cannot name,

like a sorcerer's sorcerer, like some ancient worshiper from an empty warehouse
with its roof caved in, where St. Francis's homeless birds might have found a place
to stay, some sacristy of broken staves and stones, some lost religion of loitering,
trespassing and vagrancy. She says, *That's enough for tonight now. Go home now, go home.*

And then she takes my hand, in the way that your mother would come back from
the grave and take your hand, and though I am not deserving, though I am not
deserving at all, deserving only to be forgotten, to be eternally cursed, because
the slim piece of what remains of my homeless soul could sit silently in the last pew,
the last row in the broken, bombed out Grace Evangelical Church of The Worlds
Reversed, she presses my hand, actually gives me back three wrinkled one dollar bills

that feel, for all the world, like the first leaves to fall in the last September I'll ever know.

She says, *That's enough, that's enough now, for sure. God bless you now, God bless you,*

and *God bless you, sir.*

In the Valley

Here in the Silicon, amid the constant conjuring, confabs and gonfalons,
everyone congregates at the Church of the Next to the Next Biggest Thing,
and hurries their children past the Saturday methadone clinics for ex-cons.
Here Bullshitting the Bullshitter is the First Consideration. Hustle is King.
And here, twice in the broken teeth of this week, this woman walking by,
past the Cal-Mart on Cali, this lifer, cipher, this tiny death angel drawing nigh,
her push-me-pull-you shopping carts, her black trash bags like bodies piled high,
seen and unseen, lost and found, her teeming, unseemly caravanserai.

She's shrinkwrapped herself entirely in black, head to foot, black mufti, geisha-tied,
electrical tape so precisely applied, keeping everything, even shadows, from getting inside,
her Yoko Ono glasses hide her dilated eyes, like all the cop bullet holes in *Bonnie and Clyde*,
like Abu Ghraib skies, like the abandoned underground lepers in *Ben-Hur* before Jesus died.
She lives so deep inside, like an alien alien, like Plato's lost cave, like a virgin birth.

She is the loneliest woman on the face of the earth.
How is it tonight that of all that week, of all the weeks from last July to this December,
that in this bright city, this face in the night, the woman in black is all that I remember.